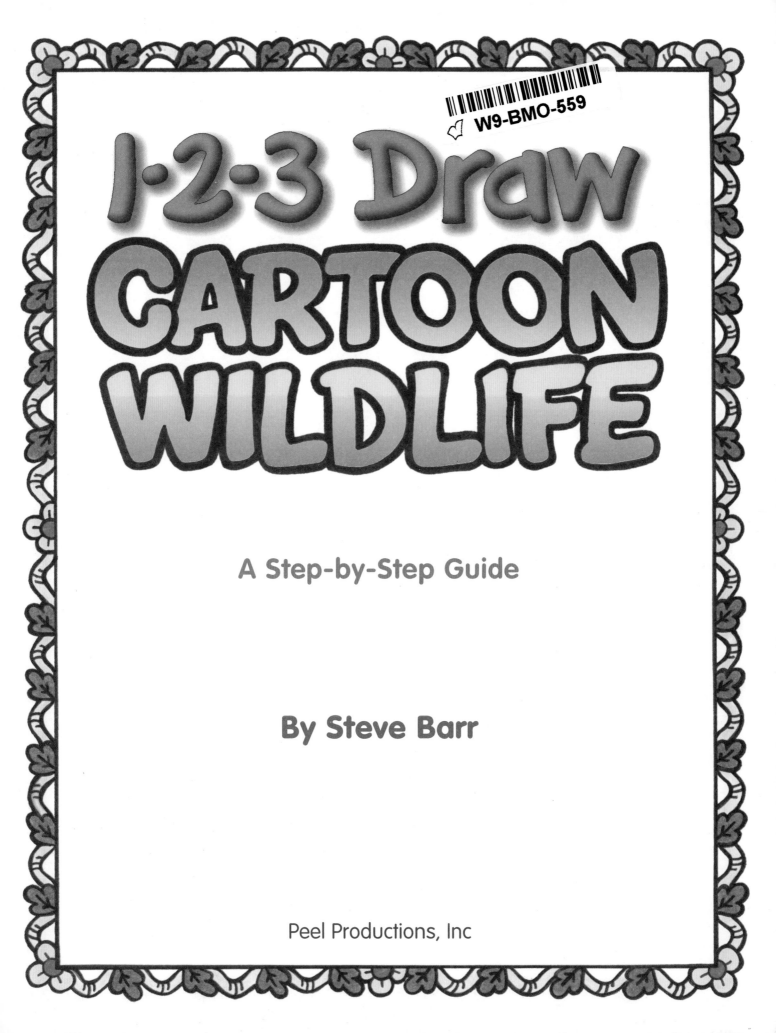

1·2·3 Draw CARTOON WILDLIFE

A Step-by-Step Guide

By Steve Barr

W9-BMO-559

Peel Productions, Inc

This book is dedicated to my friend Gina Amling,
who made writing and illustrating this book series
possible. She always makes me laugh and smile,
and I will be eternally grateful for her
companionship and encouragement.

— S.B.

Copyright ©2004 Steve Barr.
All rights reserved, including the right of reproduction in whole or in part,
in any form.
Published by Peel Productions, Inc.
Printed in China

Library of Congress Cataloging-in-Publication Data

Barr, Steve, 1958-

1-2-3 draw cartoon wildlife: a step-by-step guide / by Steve Barr.

    v. cm.

Contents: Before you begin -- Cartooning tips -- Basic shapes and
lines -- Baby bear -- Hippo -- Elephant -- Camel -- Little lion king --
Large lion -- Monkey -- Ostrich -- Tiger -- Apes -- Leopard -- Big bear -
- Polar bear.

ISBN 0-939217-70-8 (alk. paper)

1. Animals in art--Juvenile literature. 2. Cartooning--Technique--
Juvenile literature. [1. Animals in art. 2. Cartooning--Technique.] I.

Title: One-two-three draw cartoon wildlife. II. Title.

NC1764.8.A54 B375 2003

741.5--dc21   2002013520

Distributed to the trade and art
markets in North America by

NORTH LIGHT BOOKS,
an imprint of F&W Publications, Inc.
4700 East Galbraith Road
Cincinnati, OH 45236

(800) 289-0963

Table of Contents

Before you begin.

You will need the following supplies.

1. A pencil (or pencils!)
2. An eraser
3. A pencil sharpener
4. Colored pencils, markers or crayons
5. LOTS of paper
6. A good light source
7. A comfortable place to draw
8. Your imagination!

Ready?
Let's draw
cartoon wildlife!

Hint: put your drawings in a folder and save them. You will be able to see how much you improve as you sketch more and more. When you do a drawing you are really proud of, sign it and give it to a friend or family member. When they hang it on their refrigerator or somewhere else for everyone to see, you will know your cartoon made someone happy.

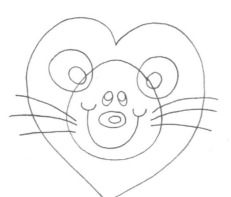

NO RULES!!!!

I think I have one of the greatest jobs in the world. I get to draw funny pictures all day long and I get paid well to do it! I am a successful cartoonist because I do it my way. There are no rules about cartooning, so you can spend hours sketching, doodling and playing with different shapes and lines to create your very own style cartoon.

Use this book as a basic guide, practice and change anything you want to make your drawing truly your own. You can make a nose as big as you want, eyes any shape you choose, and you can exaggerate anything you want. Just practice, practice, practice, and have fun. If your drawing makes you laugh or smile, you are well on your way to becoming a talented cartoonist.

1-2-3 Cartooning Tips:

1 Draw lightly at first — SKETCH!

2 Practice, practice, practice!

3 Have fun drawing cartoon wildlife!

Sketch, doodle, play!

Basic Shapes and Lines

Here are the basic shapes and lines you will use to draw cartoon wildlife:

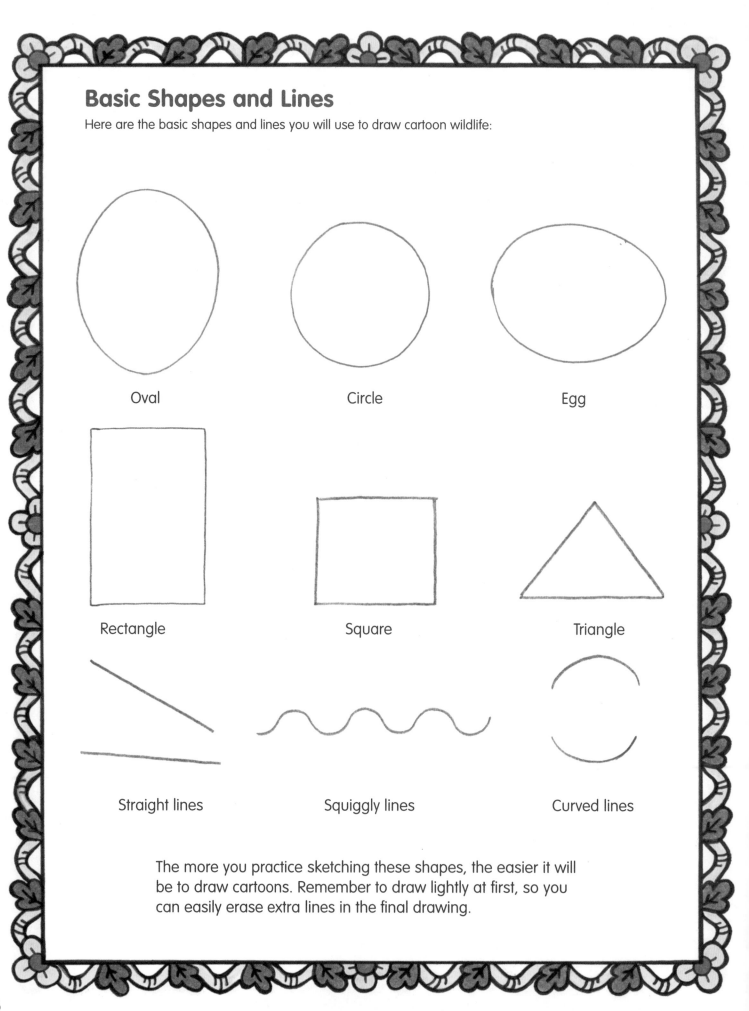

Oval

Circle

Egg

Rectangle

Square

Triangle

Straight lines

Squiggly lines

Curved lines

The more you practice sketching these shapes, the easier it will be to draw cartoons. Remember to draw lightly at first, so you can easily erase extra lines in the final drawing.

Baby bear

Let's start by drawing a baby bear. We will sketch his face first, so leave some room on your paper, below his head, to add the body.

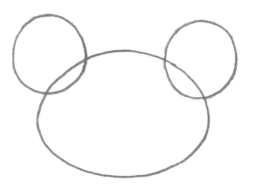

1 Sketch three overlapping ovals.

2 Sketch two small ovals (one inside the other) for the nose.

3 Sketch two small ovals for the eyes. Shade in the outside of the nose.

4 Sketch a small circle inside each ear. Shade in the outside oval of each eye. Draw a curved line for a smiling mouth.

5 Sketch a large oval for the body. Draw two curved lines for the feet.

6 LOOK at the outstretched arms and paws. Draw four straight lines for the arms and two ovals for the paws.

7 Sketch four small ovals on each hand, for fingers. Draw curved lines on his arms and body for a shirt.

8 Draw a curved line below his shirt to show his full belly. Add two curved toe lines, on each foot.

9 LOOK at the final drawing! Erase extra sketch lines. Boldly draw over the final lines. Shade and color your baby bear.

Congratulations! Beautiful baby bear!

Hippopotamus

Now let's draw a simple cartoon hippo. Remember to sketch lightly at first. We will sketch his face first, so leave some room on your paper, below his head, to add the body.

1   Sketch a large oval, for the hippo's round body. LOOK at the popcorn-shaped head. Sketch it.

2   Sketch two ovals for ears. Add two eyes and shade. Draw a curved line for a smile. Add a curved line for a tail.

3 Sketch a small circle inside each ear. Draw a curved line and a small circle for his nose. Draw four straight lines, below his body, for legs. Draw three curved lines to connect the bottoms of the legs.

4 Add curved lines for eyebrows. Draw toenails.

5 LOOK at the final drawing! Erase extra sketch lines. Boldly go over and darken the final lines. Shade and color your hippo any way you want!

Happy Hippo!

Baby elephant

Let's try our hand at drawing a baby elephant. We will sketch his face first, so leave room on your paper to add the body.

1 Sketch two overlapping ovals for the head and ear. Sketch another oval for the eye.

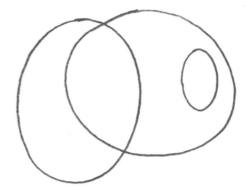

2 Draw an eyeball, inside the eye oval. Add shading. Draw two curved lines for a smile.

3 Draw a curved line for an eyebrow. Sketch two curved lines and an oval for his trunk.

4 Sketch a large oval for his body. Draw two curved lines on his trunk.

5 Using curved lines, sketch the arm shape. Add his legs.

6 Starting at the top, draw two curved lines for his hair. Draw four small ovals for his tail. Shade the tail tip ovals. Add curved lines for nails on his arm. Draw curved lines for his foot pads. Add toenails on each foot.

7 LOOK at the final drawing! Erase extra sketch lines. Boldly darken the final lines. I made my baby elephant pink. Shade and color yours any way you want. Give him polka dots or stripes if you wish.

Extraordinary elephant!

Young camel

You are catching on really fast! Let's draw a cartoon camel. We will sketch her face first, so leave some room on your paper, below her head, to add the body.

1 Sketch three overlapping ovals for the nose, head, and ear.

2 Sketch the eye and shade the eyeball.

3 Draw a curved line for her nostril. Sketch a small oval inside the ear.

4 Using curved lines, sketch her chin.

5 Draw curved lines on top of her head for hair. Add another ear. Draw curved lines for a smile. Add her eyebrow.

6 Draw two long curved lines for your camel's long neck. Sketch a large oval for the body.

7 Add a large curved line above the body for her hump. Sketch six straight lines below the body for legs.

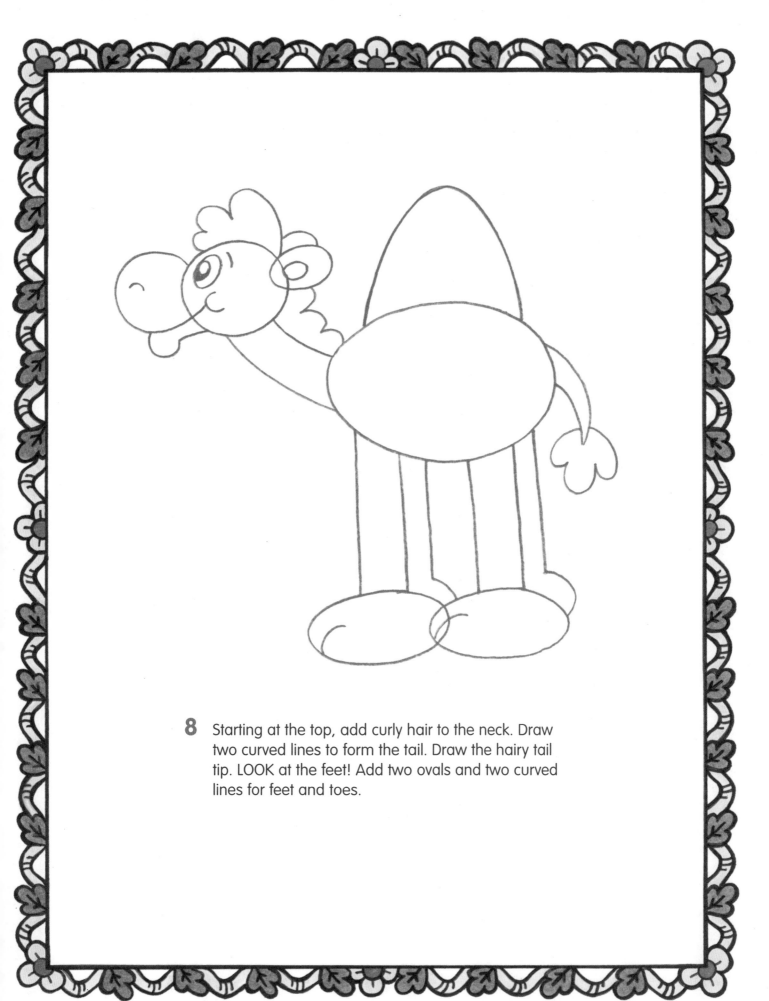

8 Starting at the top, add curly hair to the neck. Draw two curved lines to form the tail. Draw the hairy tail tip. LOOK at the feet! Add two ovals and two curved lines for feet and toes.

9 LOOK at the final drawing! Erase extra sketch lines. Go over and darken the final lines. Shade and color.

Cute camel! I love her big hump!

Little lion king

The lion is known as the king of the jungle. Let's draw a chubby little lion king.

1 Sketch three overlapping ovals for the nose, head, and ear.

2 Sketch an oval with a circle inside it, for the nose tip. Draw the eye and shade the bottom of it.

3 Draw two wavy lines for hair. Draw a small circle inside the ear oval. Shade in the nose.

4 Sketch a small curved line, below the nose for his chin. Add more wavy hair around the neck and behind the ear.

5 Starting at the top, draw the crown. Sketch an oval for his body. Sketch an overlapping oval for a foot.

6 Draw three small circles on top of his crown. Draw a curved line behind the foot oval for his other foot.

7 Draw his arm, with paw lines. Add toe lines to his feet. Draw his long tail and its fluffy tip.

8 LOOK at the final drawing! Erase extra sketch lines. Boldly go over and darken the final lines. Shade and color your lion.

His crown certainly makes him look like a king! You can give cartoon characters human characteristics by adding hats and clothes to them. We will learn more about that later in this book.

Large lion

Let's draw a grown-up lion. Sketch lightly at first and look closely at each step. Leave plenty of room below his head so we can add his body later.

1 Sketch a large valentine shape. Add three overlapping ovals for the head and ears.

2 Sketch the ovals for his eyes and nose.

3 Shade in the eyes and nose. Draw curved lines for his smiling mouth and round cheeks.

4 Sketch a small oval inside each ear. Draw three curved lines on each side of his face for big whiskers.

5 LOOK at the body circle, below his mane. Sketch it. Add straight lines for the arms and legs.

6 Sketch ovals for his hands and thumbs. Sketch two overlapping ovals for his big feet.

24

7 LOOK at the final drawing! Add finger lines to his paws. Draw toe lines on his feet. Draw his tail and his fluffy tail tip. Erase extra sketch lines. Darken the final lines. Shade and color.

GRRRREAT lion!

Monkey

Let's draw a silly cartoon monkey.

1 Sketch two overlapping ovals for the head and ear. Sketch an oval for the eye.

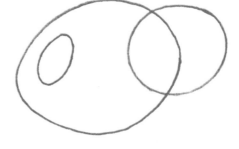

2 Sketch an oval for the nose. Sketch and shade the eyeball. Draw a small circle in his ear.

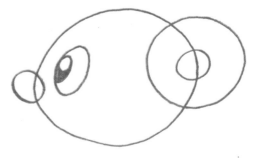

3 Draw two curved lines to form his face. Add a curved line for his other ear.

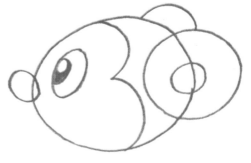

4 Sketch a curved line for his mouth. Add a curved line below his nose. Add a curved line for his cheek.

5 Sketch two overlapping ovals, below the monkey's head, for his body.

6 Draw his long curved tail.

7 LOOK at the way he is standing! Sketch four curved lines for his arms. Sketch circles for his hands. Sketch curved lines and an oval for his legs and feet.

8 Sketch small ovals for fingers on his left hand. Sketch an oval and curved lines for fingers on his right hand.

9 LOOK at the final drawing! Sketch ovals and curved lines on his feet for toes. Erase extra sketch lines. Darken the final lines. Shade and color your monkey.

Merry monkey!
You did a great job!

Ostrich

After seeing how well you drew the monkey, I am sure you will have no trouble drawing an ostrich. Remember to sketch lightly at first so you can erase later.

1 Sketch a large oval for the head. Draw an oval, with a smaller oval inside, for the eye. Darken part of the eye.

2 Draw a curved line to begin the beak. Draw another curved line on the bottom to finish the beak.

3 Draw two curved lines on the top of its head. Add a small curved line for an eyebrow. Draw two small curved lines for the mouth.

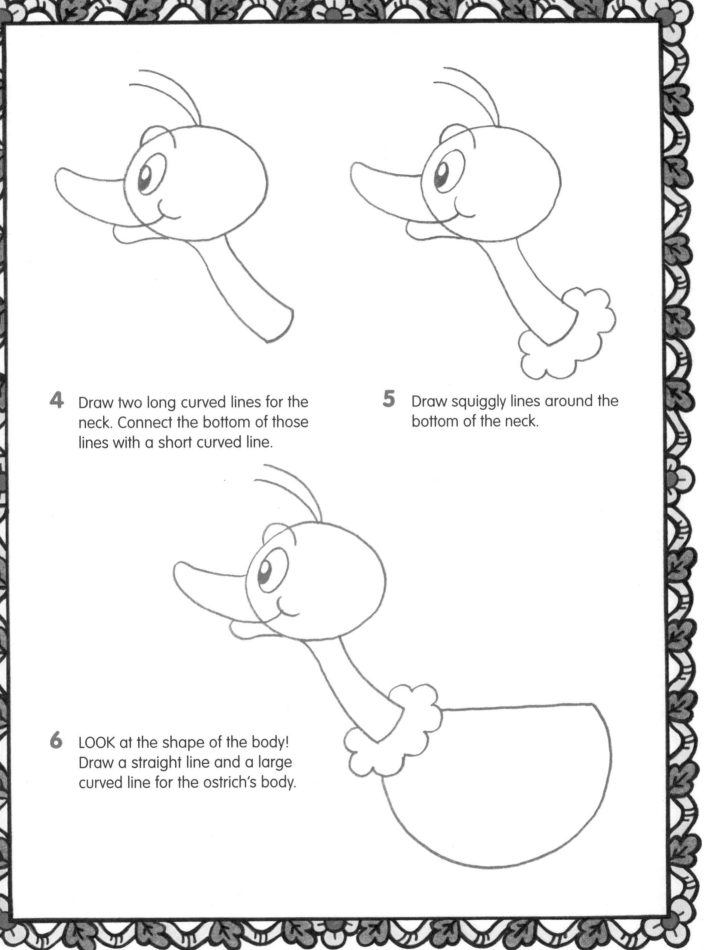

4 Draw two long curved lines for the neck. Connect the bottom of those lines with a short curved line.

5 Draw squiggly lines around the bottom of the neck.

6 LOOK at the shape of the body! Draw a straight line and a large curved line for the ostrich's body.

7 LOOK at the shape of the tail.
Draw a straight line and three
curved lines for a tail. Add a long
curved line, with two connecting
curved lines for the wing feathers.
Draw three long straight lines
below the body for legs.

8 Add an oval and a curved line for feet.

9 Add a small oval to the back of the foot. Draw curved lines on each foot for toes.

34

10 LOOK at the final drawing. Erase extra sketch lines. Add color.

Nice job!

Tiger

Let's draw a tiger. It's as easy as "1-2-3"!

1 Sketch two ovals and a curved line for the tiger's head, nose and ear.

2 Draw an oval inside an oval for the eye. Darken part of the eye.

3 Draw a small oval in his ear. Add a small oval for the nose tip. Darken part of it.

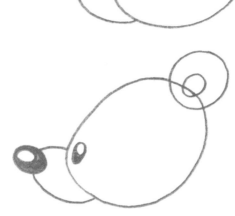

4 Draw a small curved line behind his ear, for the second ear. Draw a curved line for his mouth. Draw two curved lines, connecting in the center of his head.

5 Draw two triangles on his head, below the ears. Add three curved lines for some tiger hair.

6 Draw straight lines for the neck and upper body. Sketch an oval for his middle.

7 Add two straight lines for his arm. Draw three straight lines for his legs.

8 Sketch an oval for his hand. Draw an oval and a curved line to form his feet.

9 Add a few straight lines with a curved line on the end for a tail. Draw finger and toe lines.

10 LOOK at the final drawing! Erase extra sketch lines. Add more triangles. Color your tiger!

Ape

Let's draw a cartoon ape. There are quite a few steps to this drawing, so pay close attention to my examples and you will draw an adorable cartoon ape. Leave room to add his body after you draw the face.

1 Sketch an oval for the jaws. Sketch a small oval for the ear. Draw a curved line for the top of the head.

2 Connect the curved line to the bottom oval with a straight line. Sketch a small circle for a nose.

3 Sketch two ovals for eyes.

4 Add an oval inside each eye oval. Darken part of the eye. Draw a small oval inside the ear. Add a small curved line under the nose.

5 Draw two connecting curved lines, around the face. Add two curved lines to make a smiling mouth. Draw a curved line for his neck.

6 Sketch a large oval for his chest. Add a large curved line below that for his hips.

7 Draw two long curved lines for arms. Sketch two circles for hands.

8 Draw three short curved lines for legs. Add an oval and a curved line to each hand for fingers. Draw a curved line for a thumb on the left hand.

9 Add partial ovals, to the bottom of each leg, for feet.

10 Add a curved line to his chest. Draw curved lines on his left foot for toes.

11 LOOK at the final drawing! Erase extra sketch lines. Darken your final lines. Add color.

Wow!!!
Show this drawing to your family and friends. I bet they'll go "ape" over it!

Facial expressions

Since cartoon characters often have human traits, you need to learn how to give them human expressions. Using simple shapes and lines, for the eyes and mouth, you can change the ape's expression.

Surprised

Confused

Mad

Pick the face you like the most. Draw it! Add color.

Really glad!

Really angry!

Sad

Girl ape

Let's add a bow and beads make your ape a girl! Just follow these simple steps.

1 Draw the ape face again. (See page 39 for details.)

2 Add three lines to each eye for eyelashes.

3 Sketch three curved lines on top of her head for a bow.

4 Draw curved lines, for partial circles, to decorate the bow.

5 Draw a row of circles, around her neck, for a necklace.

6 LOOK at the final drawing! Add color.

Isn't she lovely?
You can make any of your cartoon animals look feminine by adding just a few small details like this. Try it on some of the animals you have already drawn.

Sailor ape

You can give cartoon characters their own personality just by giving them some simple clothing. Let's give the ape a sailor's hat.

1 Draw the ape's face again. (See page 39 for details.) Draw two straight lines, from the top of his head, to begin his hat.

2 Connect those lines with a curved line.

3 Add a curved line above that. Draw small curved lines on each side of his hat.

4 Draw a curved line on the hat.

5 LOOK at the final drawing! Add color.

Angry leopard

Let's draw an angry leopard. Remember to draw his head at the top of the paper and leave plenty of room for his body.

1 Sketch three ovals.

2 Draw two curved lines inside the eye oval. Draw a straight line to begin his nose.

3 Add two ovals for his nose tip. Draw a curved line to connect the nose to his face.

4 Draw a small circle in his ear. Add a curved line for his other ear. Draw a curved line across his eye. Add a small curved line for his jaw.

5 Draw a few ovals on his face for spots.

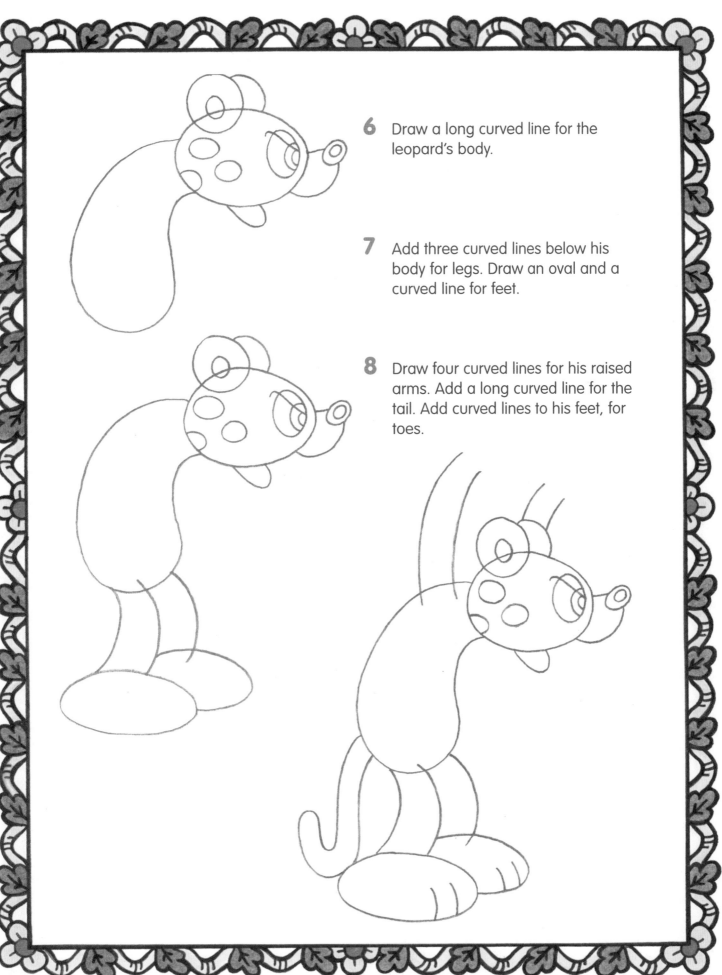

6 Draw a long curved line for the leopard's body.

7 Add three curved lines below his body for legs. Draw an oval and a curved line for feet.

8 Draw four curved lines for his raised arms. Add a long curved line for the tail. Add curved lines to his feet, for toes.

9 Sketch an oval at the end of each arm, for hands. Add ovals and curved lines to his body for leopard spots.

10 Sketch four ovals on each hand for fingers. Most cartoon characters only have four fingers, counting their thumbs. If you would rather draw five fingers on each hand, feel free. It's your leopard.

11 LOOK at the final drawing! Erase extra sketch lines. Darken your final lines. Add color.

GREAT JOB!

Big bear

Remember the first cartoon character you drew when you started this book? It was a cute little baby bear. Let's draw a grown-up bear now.

1   Sketch two ovals.

2   Draw a straight line and a curved line for the nose. Draw an oval for the eye. Darken part of it.

3   Draw an oval for his nose tip. Darken part of it. Add a curved line for the mouth.

4   Add a curved line to the mouth line for a pudgy cheek. Draw a curved line for the chin. Draw a small circle inside his ear.

5   Put two curved lines on top of his head.

6 Sketch a large oval for the body. Draw two curved lines, from the head to the body, for the bear's neck.

7 Sketch a large oval inside his body for an arm. Sketch three ovals for fingers. Add a small oval for his tail.

8 Draw three curved lines for legs. Sketch an oval and a curved line for feet.

9 Add curved lines to his feet for toes.

10 LOOK at the final drawing! Erase extra sketch lines. Add a few curved lines to make him look hairy. Darken your final lines. Add color.

OR...

If you want to make him a polar bear, go around the outside of his body with curved lines to make him look fluffy. Leave him white and just shade around the outside of his fur with a light blue pencil or crayon.

Cool!
You just learned how to draw two different bears in the same lesson!

Polar bear

Let's draw another polar bear. This one is going to be really cool. We are going to dress him for a tropical trip. Are you ready? Let's draw!

1   Sketch an oval for the head. Sketch two ovals for the ear.

2   Add an oval for the eye. Draw another oval inside the eye. Darken part of it. Draw a straight line to begin the nose.

3   Draw a connecting curved line to finish the nose. Add a curved line for the chin.

4   Draw an oval for the nose tip. Darken part of it.

5   Draw two curved lines for the smiling mouth.

6 Draw two curved lines for his neck.

7 Sketch a large oval for the bear's body.

8 Sketch an oval for his arm. Sketch a small oval for his tail.

9 Sketch ovals for his fingers. Draw three curved lines for his legs. (He is going to be sitting down.) Add an oval and a curved line for his feet.

10 Draw two straight lines and a curved line on his neck for his collar. Put a curved line in the middle of his arm for a sleeve. Draw curved lines on his feet for toes.

11 Sketch a long oval on the top of his head to begin his hat. Draw curved lines to make his glasses. Draw two curved lines on his body for his shirt.

12 Add two straight lines and a curved line to finish his hat. Add a jagged line and a curved line for the collar and shirt on the left side of his body.

13 LOOK at the final drawing! Erase extra sketch lines. Darken your final lines. Add a few flowers and circles to his shirt. Add color.

He sure looks happy to be in the tropics.

Hippo girl

Let's draw a hippo girl. We'll draw her head and body first, then add clothes and accessories.

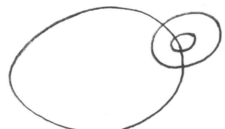

1   Sketch an oval for the head. Sketch two ovals for the ear.

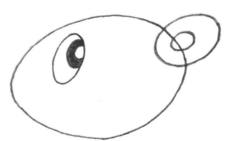

2   Draw two ovals for the eye. Darken part of the inside oval.

3   Draw a curved line above and below the eye. Add a curved line for her horn. Sketch a small curved line below the horn to begin her mouth.

4   Draw two curved lines for her smile. Sketch an oval below her head for the body.

5   Draw curved lines for her arms.

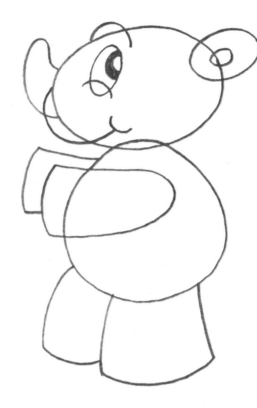

6 Draw curved lines for legs.

7 Add small curved lines to arms and feet for toenails. Add a curved line for a tail.

8 Erase extra sketch lines. Darken final lines.

9 Draw two triangles and a circle on top of her head to make a bow. Draw three straight lines on her eye for lashes. Add a curved neck line. Draw a row of small circles on her wrist for a pearl bracelet. Add a curved line at her waist. Draw curved lines for her skirt.

10 LOOK at her purse! Draw the curved and straight lines you see for the purse.

11 LOOK at the final drawing! Erase extra sketch lines. Darken the final lines. Color your hippo.

She's hip and happy! Good job!

Use what you have learned in this book to create cartoon wildlife of your very own. Draw two or three different characters and put them together in a scene. Here we have the lion drawing the bear.

Award yourself! On the next page you'll find an award certificate you can photocopy to let the world know you're a **Cartoonist's Apprentice First Class!**

Have you enjoyed this book?

Find out about other books in this series and see sample pages online at

www.123draw.com

THIS IS TO CERTIFY THAT
THE TITLE OF

Wildlife Cartoonist's Apprentice

HAS BEEN AWARDED TO

NAME: _____

FOR THE SUCCESSFUL COMPLETION
OF "1-2-3 DRAW CARTOON WILDLIFE"

Date: _____

Signed: *Steve Barr*
(INSTRUCTOR)